Horrid History of Beauty

MURDEROUS MAKE-UP

ANITA CROY

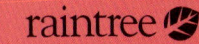

a Capstone company — publishers for children

Raintree is an imprint of Capstone Global Library Limited, a company incorporated in England and Wales having its registered office at 264 Banbury Road, Oxford, OX2 7DY – Registered company number: 6695582

www.raintree.co.uk
myorders@raintree.co.uk

Text © Capstone Global Library Limited 2020
The moral rights of the proprietor have been asserted.

All rights reserved. No part of this publication may be reproduced in any form or by any means (including photocopying or storing it in any medium by electronic means and whether or not transiently or incidentally to some other use of this publication) without the written permission of the copyright owner, except in accordance with the provisions of the Copyright, Designs and Patents Act 1988 or under the terms of a licence issued by the Copyright Licensing Agency, Barnard's Inn, 86 Fetter Lane, London, EC4A 1EN (www.cla.co.uk). Applications for the copyright owner's written permission should be addressed to the publisher.

Originated by Capstone Global Library Ltd
Printed and bound in India

ISBN 978 1 4747 7766 7 (hardback)
ISBN 978 1 4747 7769 8 (paperback)

British Library Cataloguing in Publication Data
A full catalogue record for this book is available from the British Library.

Acknowledgements
We would like to thank the following for permission to reproduce photographs:
Cover: Shutterstock: Juri Pozzi; Inside: Library of Congress: Esther Bubley: p. 36; Shutterstock: ArgenLant: p. 7b; Steve Boice: p. 13; S. Borisov: p. 20; Buenaventura: p. 4b; DavidRebata: p. 23t; Elnavegante: p.21b; Everett – Art: pp. 22, 27b; Vitalii Hulai: p. 17; K. Jensen: p. 31t; Julianne.hide: p. 43b; Kaetana: p.5; B.S.Karan: p. 7t; Kostiantyn Kravchenko: p. 43t; LiliGraphie: p. 33t; Mountainpix: p. 6; NemesisINC: p. 19; Northfoto: p. 37; Juri Pozzi: p. 24; Lorna Roberts: p. 39; Renata Sedmakova: p. 11; Spflaum: p. 40; IR Stone: p. 33b; Kuttelvaserova Stuchelova: p. 21t; Maksim Toome: p. 41; Liliya Vantsura: p. 4c; Gorbash Varvara: p. 32; Wavebreakmedia: p. 42; Vladimir Wrangel: p. 8; Wikimedia Commons: pp. 9t, 15, 3; B. Altman & Co.: p. 27t; Andrea Appiani: p. 30; Daniel Bachler: p. 25; Bain News Service: p. 34; François Boucher: p. 23b; Fabien Dany - www.fabiendany.com: p. 10; Don English; Paramount Pictures: p. 35b; Marcus Gheeraerts the Younger: pp. 1, 17t; formerly attributed to George Gower: p. 16; Jean-Pierre Houël: p. 26; Petar Miloševic: p. 14; Pattych: p. 12; Dante Gabriel Rossetti: p. 31b; Peter Paul Rubens: p. 18; R. Sayer & J. Bennett: p. 28; Llann Wé: p. 38; Time Inc., Metro-Goldwyn-Mayer photograph by Harvey White: p. 35t.

Every effort has been made to contact copyright holders of material reproduced in this book. Any omissions will be rectified in subsequent printings if notice is given to the publisher.

All the internet addresses (URLs) given in this book were valid at the time of going to press. However, due to the dynamic nature of the internet, some addresses may have changed, or sites may have changed or ceased to exist since publication. While the author and publisher regret any inconvenience this may cause readers, no responsibility for any such changes can be accepted by either the author or the publisher.

CONTENTS

Chapter 1
ANCIENT MAKE-UP 4
EARLY SOCIETIES 6
EGYPTIAN BEAUTIES 8
PAINTED FACES 10
WAR PAINT 12

Chapter 2
THE MIDDLE AGES 14
THE IMAGE OF ROYALTY 16

Chapter 3
THE EARLY MODERN WORLD 18
DEADLY ITALIANS 20
THE FRENCH CONNECTION 22
GEISHA 24

Chapter 4
THE NINETEENTH CENTURY 26
THE DANDY 28
PAINTED LADIES 30

Chapter 5
THE TWENTIETH CENTURY 32
HOORAY FOR HOLLYWOOD 34
AVON CALLING! 36
POWER OF POP 38

Chapter 6
THE TWENTY-FIRST CENTURY 40
WHAT'S INSIDE? 42

TIMELINE 44
GLOSSARY 46
FIND OUT MORE 47
INDEX 48

Chapter 1

ANCIENT
- MAKE-UP -

Make-up is as old as humanity. Since prehistoric times, men and women have painted their faces as make-up has gone in and out of fashion.

No one knows when people started wearing make-up – but it was very early in human history.

MAGICAL COLOUR

Some of our oldest prehistoric ancestors seem to have used make-up to protect themselves as they hunted animals and gathered roots and berries. They painted their faces and bodies with colour to give them a feeling of security. Perhaps they believed, for example, that they could capture some of the power of the Sun by painting their skin yellow. Or people may have believed that painting designs on their faces would scare off any enemies they might meet – or any evil spirits. **Neolithic** people buried their dead with red ochre, so the colour was probably thought to have a magical power. Coloured skin helped to protect both the living and the dead.

Ochre was used to make a wide range of yellows, reds, oranges and browns.

Ancient peoples also used ochre to paint handprints on the walls of caves.

[4]

Make-up also had a practical purpose. As early humans' faces and bodies became less covered with hair, layers of colour helped protect their skin from the wind and the sun.

The Neanderthals, close relatives of humans who lived around 50,000 years ago, also painted their faces. Archaeologists in Spain have found seashells that were used as pots to hold reddish, yellow and black coloured powders. The make-up was made from berries and clay.

DECORATION

Once early peoples settled down in permanent villages and began to develop civilizations, they began to use make-up for decoration rather than for protection. The make-up was still made from natural products such as berries and clay, but also from a range of other **minerals**. These minerals were ground into powder and then mixed with water or oil to form a paste that could be painted onto the skin. Some people pricked colour into their skin to form permanent tattoos.

Dancing girls in India wore make-up from early times.

[5]

EARLY SOCIETIES

Many ancient peoples loved using make-up. For fashionable Egyptians, for example, painting their faces was part of their daily routine.

The Sumerians of Mesopotamia are famous for inventing writing, the wheel and other innovations. They were also among the first developed cultures to start using make-up.

ANCIENT MESOPOTAMIA

In a 5,000-year-old Sumerian tomb near Ur, in present-day Iraq, archaeologists have found a pot containing blue-green malachite, a mineral used as eye shadow, and a **cosmetics** case of equipment such as tweezers. They also found lip colour used over 4,000 years ago by a Sumerian queen called Schub-ad.

The ancient Egyptians painted their eyes because they believed the eyes revealed a person's soul.

Assyrian warriors went into battle with large, square beards, pink cheeks and dark eyeliner.

The Assyrians were descendants of the Sumerians. They painted their faces with white lead to make their skin appear paler. King Assurbanipal, who lived in the seventh century BC, wore **rouge** on his cheeks, dark paint called **kohl** on his eyes and perfume all over his body.

After Sumer and Assyria, make-up spread through the ancient world. The Romans adopted Egyptian beauty routines into their bathing rituals. The Minoans of Crete, however, made their own make-up using beeswax, honey, olive oil and tree **resin**.

Obsidian was so useful that it was traded over long distances in the ancient world.

to die for

Ancient peoples had no mirrors to help them apply make-up. They probably asked someone else to put it on for them. By 6000 BC, people used a smooth black stone called obsidian to make mirrors. Later, they used stone, bronze and other metals such as copper. This meant that they could finally check their make-up properly.

[7]

EGYPTIAN
- BEAUTIES -

Ancient Egypt was home to women whose beauty is still legendary today, such as Queen Cleopatra. But many Egyptian men used make-up, too.

Ancient Egyptians cared about their appearance. Rich Egyptians used oils, pastes and lotions to keep their skin soft. They didn't realize that many of the cosmetics they used were slowly poisoning them.

THE EYES HAVE IT

The Egyptians believed the eyes revealed a person's soul, so both men and women used make-up to emphasize their eyes. They outlined their eyes with thick black lines. The lines were either drawn using kohl, a black powder made by grinding **antimony**, **manganese** and **lead**, or using crushed ants' eggs. The lines extended from the corners of the eyes, making the eyes seem larger.

This bust of Queen Nefertiti shows how a fashionable Egyptian woman would have looked over 3,350 years ago.

A MAKE-UP ROUTINE

Ancient Egyptian women put on make-up using a "see face" (mirror). They used stone slabs called palettes to grind up minerals into powder for make-up, and kept creams and lotions in bronze jars. Popular lotions included face creams made from egg whites or quince, as well as **lead carbonate**. Women outlined their eyes in kohl, and coloured the area between their upper eyelids and eyebrows using red or green eyeshadow. They applied orange lipstick, and used a yellow-red dye made from henna to colour their fingernails and toenails. Putting on all this make-up took many hours – but they would have had slaves to help them.

Egyptians used decorated stone slabs called palettes to grind up minerals into powder for make-up.

to die for

Throughout history, wealthy people have wanted to look different from poor people. In Egypt, rich women painted their faces lily white so they stood out from people who worked outdoors. However, they used a powder of lead carbonate – a deadly poison. Kohl also contained a high proportion of lead. The mineral slowly poisoned the stylish people who wore it.

Dancers and musicians have their eyes outlined in kohl in this painting from an Egyptian tomb.

[9]

PAINTED - FACES -

After the ancient Egyptians set a trend for glamorous make-up, the ancient Greeks adopted a more natural look.

The Romans admired the Egyptian queen Cleopatra, with her highly painted face, but they also admired the natural appearance of the Greeks. Roman make-up was somewhere between the two.

PALE BUT INTERESTING

In ancient Greece, around the sixth to fourth centuries BC, men saw women's role as being modest homemakers. Women were expected to stay indoors, spending their time weaving clothes. Unlike women in ancient Egypt, Greek women had to appear modest and pure. For make-up, they followed an approach of "less is more". To achieve the look, they used a highly **toxic** mix of white lead and chalk to whiten their faces. They mixed a root from Syria called puperissium with vinegar to colour their cheeks. They did not paint their eyes.

A servant holds up a mirror for a Roman woman to check her make-up.

[10]

Greek men, meanwhile, covered their bodies with oils and perfume and used rouge and lip colour.

MAKE-UP IN ROME

The Romans **imported** Egyptian make-up, and traded it throughout the Roman Empire. They also made their own make-up from substances such as toxic antimony for eyeliner and non-toxic wood ash and **saffron** for black-and-gold eye shadow. They showed off any blue veins in their skin by painting them with blue paint. However, freckles were considered undesirable, so the Romans lightened them using a paste of ground wheat mixed with lemon.

Jezebel sits on her throne. "Jezebel" became a term for a **vain** woman.

hello beautiful

In the ninth century BC, a Phoenician princess called Jezebel married Ahab, the prince of Israel. Jezebel wore a lot of make-up and beautiful clothes. After she persuaded her husband to abandon the worship of an Israeli god, the Israelis condemned her as a "painted lady". She is said to have met a horrible death, having been thrown to the dogs and killed.

[11]

WAR
- PAINT -

Warriors have always painted their faces and bodies to scare their enemies and to show which side they belong to.

Long before ancient peoples had the idea of painting their faces to look attractive, warriors painted their faces in order to appear more frightening.

ANCIENT WARFARE

From around 1200 BC, the Assyrians decided that women should cover their faces with **veils** while men, including warriors, painted their cheeks red and put on eye make-up. They also used perfume so that they smelled nice as they went into battle.

Much later, the ancient Britons painted their faces and bodies with a blue colouring made from the woad plant. Queen Boudicca, the ruler of the Iceni tribe, fought against the Romans in Britain in AD 60. She ordered her warriors to paint their faces blue before battle. The Iceni managed to defeat the Romans twice before finally being defeated themselves.

This pot from ancient Peru shows a Moche warrior with his face painted for battle.

WAR PAINT IN AMERICA

Some of the best-known warriors who painted their faces came from Native American tribes. Each tribe had its own distinctive markings, with shapes and symbols that had a specific meaning. The Lakota Sioux painted black stripes on their faces, for example. The stripes indicated the warrior's role. A warrior who led a war party had two black stripes running from the corner of his eye on his right cheek. Warriors did not only use make-up to scare their enemies – it was also used in ceremonial dances and religious **rituals**.

Native Americans still use traditional make-up for ceremonial occasions.

hello beautiful

In the seventh century BC, the Babylonians ruled Mesopotamia. Their king, Nebuchadnezzar, wore make-up and told his warriors to do the same. One warrior, Parsondes, complained that make-up was not manly. As a punishment, the king forced him to shave his beard and paint his face. The result was so good that Parsondes became famous as the most beautiful woman in Babylon!

[13]

Chapter 2
THE MIDDLE
- AGES -

The Middle Ages lasted from about 500 to 1500. At this time, people left their faces unpainted, their hair uncut and their bodies unwashed. Yuck!

After the fall of Rome in 476, Christianity increased its influence throughout Europe. Christian teaching gave people a negative view of make-up.

A CHRISTIAN WORLD

Early Christian writers argued that wearing make-up showed that a person was trying to improve upon God's creation. They also said that make-up hid a person's real face. This made it a form of deception, which was a sin. Using make-up to make yourself look more attractive was a sign of vanity – which was another sin. Christian women could no longer paint their faces. If they ever dared to wear make-up, it had to look as natural as possible to honour God's work.

The Byzantine empress Theodora met her husband, Emperor Justinian, when she appeared in a beauty contest.

PALE IS BEAUTIFUL

Medieval women were expected to stay indoors. A pale skin was a sign that a woman was so wealthy she never had to go outside. To remain as pale as possible, women protected their faces outdoors with a veil. Empress Zoe was reputed to be the most beautiful woman in the Byzantine Empire. She protected her skin by never going outside.

CULTURAL EXCHANGE

Cosmetics had almost vanished from Europe before they were reintroduced by an unlikely source: warfare. In 1095 European Christians launched a series of wars against Muslims in the Holy Land. These Crusades lasted nearly 200 years and failed to conquer the Holy Land. However, they did introduce new fashions in make-up. The Crusaders returned from Asia with perfume, rouge and glass mirrors, which were common in the Islamic world. They also copied the Arabs by shaving their faces, ending the fashion for men wearing beards.

In the 1500s, Catherine de' Medici brought Italian ideas about beauty to France when she became queen there.

THE IMAGE OF
- ROYALTY -

Elizabeth I was queen of England from 1558 to 1603, a period of peace and prosperity. She gave her name to the Elizabethan Age.

Elizabeth was known as the "virgin queen", because she never married. Not that that made her less vain. Like her father, King Henry VIII, Elizabeth paid great attention to making sure her appearance was perfectly "royal".

LOOKING THE PART

Elizabeth dressed luxuriously from a young age. When she was queen, she owned 80 wigs, 27 fans and more than 3,000 dresses. It took her ladies-in-waiting four hours every day to get the queen ready. As she lost her looks, it was said that she refused to look in a mirror for the last 20 years of her life.

Like her father, Elizabeth used her appearance to project an image of power and authority.

DAMAGING MAKE-UP

To cover her skin and make her appear as pale as possible, Elizabeth was painted with layers of **ceruse**. This was made from white lead mixed with vinegar. She also used ceruse to cover her neck and hands. However, the white lead meant that the ceruse damaged her skin. One Elizabethan said that it dried the flesh and warned that: "Those women who use it about their faces do quickly become withered and grey headed."

Elizabeth's appearance was completed by orange wigs, plucked eyebrows and scarlet lips. Her eyes were outlined with kohl. Where her dress exposed her skin, the veins were outlined in blue.

Elizabeth's lips were painted with plant dye and beeswax.

to die for

The whiter a Renaissance woman's skin, the better. Some women went to great lengths to achieve a pale appearance. This included applying **leeches** to their ears. The animals would suck the blood from the women's heads, leaving them looking deathly pale.

leech

[17]

Chapter 3

THE EARLY
- MODERN WORLD -

In the Renaissance, Europe's rulers grew more fashion conscious. They ignored church teachings and used make-up to show off their wealth and status.

After the death of Elizabeth I in 1603, cosmetics became more subtle. Male make-up was generally more subtle than female make-up. Men simply added a touch of rouge to their cheeks or colour to their lips.

FRENCH STYLE

Across the English Channel in France, major changes were underway. In 1643 King Louis XIV came to the throne. During a reign of 72 years, the new king turned France into Europe's dominant political power and its undisputed leader of style and fashion.

King Louis XIII of France, the father of Louis XIV, used make-up to achieve a look his subjects found a little too feminine for a ruler!

Louis removed his **courtiers'** political power, so they spent all their time preening and following fashion. Costumes and make-up grew ever more outrageous.

WEARING PATCHES

In the 1600s an unusual beauty craze from France swept across Europe: the wearing of "patches". People began sticking small dots of black taffeta onto their faces in order to hide blemishes and scars. The patches were not harmful, but they soon became more excessive. People began to use all types of fabrics and shapes, such as crescent-shaped pieces of velvet or red silk stars.

A visitor to the court in Berlin in 1616 reported that ladies there were so heavily patched that they looked as if they had been in a fight. The black patches were not very flattering. From a distance they looked more like fleas and insects stuck to people's faces – not the look their wearers were hoping to achieve!

The shape and position of patches (shown here on a present day model) carried messages about a woman's availability for marriage.

[19]

DEADLY
- ITALIANS -

Italy could be deadly for beautiful people in the sixteenth and seventeenth centuries. Toxic face powders were just one of the dangers.

By the sixteenth century Venice was the leading city of Europe. Its location on the Adriatic Sea meant it controlled sea routes to the Middle East and Asia. As a result, every new spice and perfume coming into Europe arrived in Venice first.

VENETIAN CERUSE

Venice was the playground of the rich. Endless parties and balls took their toll on people's looks, so "more is more" became the rule for cosmetics. Heavy make-up hid the worst of the damage.

Venice had a reputation for importing the most luxurious and expensive make-up — just right for its constant partying.

to die for

In England in the late 1700s, dark eyebrows were all the rage. However, the use of lead-based cosmetics caused many women to lose their eyebrows. Instead, they made false eyebrows from mouse fur. The only problem was keeping the eyebrows glued in place. More than one woman found her eyebrows in her teacup!

Venetian ceruse was used to whiten the face and hide wrinkles. Venetian ceruse was more expensive than ordinary ceruse – but it was just as deadly. The lead in the ceruse was toxic.

INHERITANCE POWDERS

For around 50 years in the seventeenth century, dressing tables in Italy were particularly dangerous. Fashionable women could buy a clear liquid to store among their cosmetics. This Aqua Tofana was sold as "inheritance powders", and the purchaser received secret instructions on how to use it from its maker, Giulia Tofana. The bottle contained **arsenic** mixed with lead and belladonna, made from the deadly nightshade plant. Just four doses of between four and six drops of the liquid were enough to kill a man. Undetectable on the victim, the "cosmetic" was the perfect murder weapon for an unhappy wife. After more than 600 women killed their husbands with arsenic poisoning, Tofana was finally arrested and executed.

A lot of make-up was toxic, but Aqua Tofana was deadly!

[21]

THE FRENCH
- CONNECTION -

In 1682, King Louis XIV moved his court to a vast palace at Versailles just outside Paris, where he perfected his approach to fashion.

Unlike the English, who seldom bathed, King Louis XIV liked to bathe every day and he liked to smell nice.

SCENT OF POWER

Perfume-making became big business. It was part of a lavish court lifestyle where appearance was everything. Life at Versailles was so boring for courtiers with no political role that they concentrated on the way they looked. The king dressed in the finest clothes and powdered his hair grey, so his courtiers followed his lead. Powdered hair was all the rage for men, while women rouged their cheeks and wore bright lipstick. Being a "painted lady" in France was seen as a compliment. Across the English Channel, it was an insult.

The French queen Marie Antoinette was famous for buying lots of clothes and make-up.

[22]

SPEND, SPEND, SPEND

Although many people in France were poor, the court at Versailles grew more luxurious. Louis XV's daughter-in-law, Marie Antoinette, wife of Louis XVI, spent 258,000 livres on her appearance in a year – the equivalent of millions of pounds today. That bought her a huge wardrobe and every imaginable cosmetic, plus "simple" country fragrances created just for her. When the French Revolution came in 1789, such excesses led to Marie Antoinette and her husband, Louis XVI, being executed. The age of excess was over.

The palace at Versailles was the centre of Europe's fashion scene.

hello Beautiful

Madame de Pompadour was the most important of Louis XIV's mistresses. A famous beauty, she set many fashion trends. She never appeared in public without rouge on her cheeks. Her favourite shade became known as "Pompadour Pink". Even on her deathbed, her last act was to rouge her cheeks before she died.

GEISHA

It was not only Europeans who wanted to look as pale as possible. In China and Japan, there was a tradition of using make-up to whiten the skin.

The fashion for pale skins in China and Japan started early. During the second half of the sixth century, rouge, face whitener and other cosmetics reached Japan from China. It was not until AD 692, when a Buddhist priest made a lead-based face whitener for the Empress Jito, that Japan began its own trends in cosmetics.

WHITE AS A SHEET

During the Heian Period, from 794 to 1185, Japan cut its ties with the rest of the world. Women at the Imperial Court in Kyoto created their own ideas about beauty. Their ideals included a heavily whitened face and neck, shaved eyebrows, bright red lips – and blackened teeth. The look might not have been to everyone's taste!

A geisha's even white make-up helps focus the viewer's attention on the eyes and mouth.

to die for

Geisha used the white, lead-based powder that pleased the Empress Jito for centuries, but it scarred their faces – and even killed them. The powder caused skin problems and hair loss. As their skin worsened, the geisha used more powder to cover the damage. It was only in the late 1800s that rice powder replaced the deadly lead powder, and the geisha lived to tell the story.

A geisha's **kimono** is low at the back to reveal the white paint at the nape of the neck.

THE GEISHA

The appearance of the women of the Heian court influenced the tradition of the geisha. These formal female entertainers are skilled in arts such as dance and conversation, so they can entertain their male clients. They change their appearance and make-up as they are trained to become more senior geishas.

Geisha cover their face and neck with really thick white powder, paint in black eyebrows and wear bright red lipstick. The white powder is mixed with water and then applied by hand all over the face, including over the eyebrows and lips. The black eyebrows are then drawn in place before the red lips are drawn over the mouth.

[25]

Chapter 4
THE NINETEENTH
- CENTURY -

In the 1800s, the highly painted look was no longer in fashion. Now most women wanted a natural look, like Queen Victoria.

The 1789 French Revolution brought to an end the excesses of the nobles and the royal family. Across Europe, countries no longer had the money to keep such extravagant royal courts.

MEN AND WOMEN

In England, the nineteenth century saw contrasting attitudes. For men, vanity was "in", and beautifully dressed **dandies** took centre stage. They followed the lead of the trend setter, Beau Brummel. Women got the short straw, because Queen Victoria, who ruled Britain for 64 years from 1837, did not like make-up. She did not use it and even frowned upon it.

The French Revolution introduced a complete change in attitudes towards make-up in Europe.

In the United States, a plain appearance was the way to go. This was mainly in reaction to the heavily powdered hair of Britain's King George III. He had become a symbol of **oppression** during the eighteenth century and the American Revolution (1765–1783). Following the Revolution, American appearances had become far plainer.

MAKE-UP ON SALE

The little make-up that Victorian women wore was still made from natural products such as beeswax, rosewater or belladonna. Belladonna was used to open the pupils and make the eyes appear larger – even though it was deadly poisonous.

People no longer had to make their own cosmetics at home. Now cosmetics could be bought at the pharmacy. By the 1840s, many chemists in the United States employed a cosmetician. They didn't just advise women about make-up. They also covered up the black eyes of men who had been injured in fights. The first "making-up" department appeared in B. Altman's shop in New York City in 1867. Assistants taught women how to apply blusher, powder and eye make-up in a subtle and natural way.

Department stores, such as the B. Altman department store in New York City, USA, began selling make-up during the 1860s.

As a young woman, Queen Victoria was considered a great beauty. She later lost her interest in fashion.

[27]

THE DANDY

The nineteenth century saw two types of ideal male figure in a fight to the death: the dandy in one corner and the action-man in the other!

The dandy saw physical appearance as everything. Just as women were having to embrace the natural look with pale skin and just a hint of rouge, men appeared so perfectly that they were anything but natural.

THE DANDIES

The leading dandy was Beau Brummel, a friend of the Prince Regent, the heir to the British throne. Beau never appeared in public without being perfectly groomed. He claimed to spend five hours a day **coiffing** his hair, applying paste to his face to conceal blemishes and shaping his eyebrows until he looked perfect. The Prince Regent ditched his heavy make-up and copied Beau — and everyone else copied the heir to the throne.

An early form of dandy, called the Macaronis, had exaggerated hairstyles.

[28]

ACTION-MEN

The Napoleonic Wars, fought between Britain and France from 1803 to 1815, set a new male fashion. Men in uniform were everywhere. The slightly feminine dandy was replaced by a more "rugged" look. In Britain, the new popular heroes were the admirals, generals and soldiers who were fighting the French. At home, men started to copy these action-men and stopped wearing pastes and face paints. Instead they set out to look more masculine: beards and moustaches were back in and make-up was out.

The Prince Regent later became King George IV.

to die for

Across the Atlantic Ocean, American men had already moved away from the powdered and perfumed look, and had completely rejected cosmetics. In fact, the Americans' distrust of make-up was so strong that if a man used it, his reputation could be ruined. When it was discovered that the eighth US president, Martin Van Buren, used cosmetic creams, the scandal helped to end his political career.

[29]

PAINTED
- LADIES -

For women in nineteenth-century Britain, actresses and bohemians took on Queen Victoria in the make-up stakes. Who would win?

Queen Victoria's hatred of make-up was so great that she condemned painted faces as vulgar and unladylike. Many people seemed to agree with her.

NATURAL LOOK

Most women tried to appear as if they wore hardly any make-up. The French Empress Josephine, wife of Emperor Napoleon, spent hours applying her make-up to make it look as if she wasn't wearing any! Pale skin was fashionable. It implied wealth because pale-skinned women did not go out to work. Women paled their faces with chalks and powders and stayed out of the sun. They got a bit of colour by pinching their cheeks to draw blood into the skin.

Empress Josephine was one of Europe's most famous beauties.

FACE PAINTING

By the end of the nineteenth century, everything had changed. Actresses had worn make-up for centuries, but the stage had been seen as **disreputable**. Now, however, the theatre became fashionable. Even respectable women wanted to wear make-up to look like famous actresses such as Sarah Bernhardt. As the century ended, **commercial** make-up became widely available. In 1884, the French company Guerlain produced the first lipstick. Made from deer fat, beeswax and castor oil, it was wrapped in silk paper so that it did not colour the user's fingers.

By 1900, bolder colours of make-up were back in style.

hello Beautiful

From the mid-1800s, **Pre-Raphaelite** artists painted models, such as Jane Morris and Lizzie Siddal, with tumbling hair, pale faces and painted lips. This began the "Romantic" look that hasn't gone out of fashion since. Cosmetics gave a natural appearance that thousands of women copied.

Chapter 5
THE TWENTIETH
- CENTURY -

When Queen Victoria died in 1901, so did her disapproval of make-up. Thanks to changes in the United States, cosmetics were soon everywhere.

From early in the twentieth century, it was clear that the United States would lead the way in all things cosmetic. Before the United States took control, however, other forces were at work.

ALL CHANGE

In 1909 a modern Russian dance group called the Ballet Russes arrived in Paris. With the dancers' brightly coloured costumes and painted faces, the Russian ballet caused a storm. Their modern look was an instant hit. A few years later in Britain, women marching for the right to vote caused outrage by wearing red lipstick. At that time, lipstick had only really been worn by actresses or disreputable women. It was clear that the Victorian age was well and truly gone.

Young women known as **Flappers** broke the rules with their short hair and bright lipstick.

THE MODERN ERA

The place of modern make-up was cemented by the coming of the Flappers in the 1920s. These young, urban women broke many rules. Not only did they wear short skirts and have their hair cut into a bob, but they also openly wore make-up. Since World War I (1914–1918), many women had worked and earned their own money. They wanted to spend it on luxuries such as make-up. Companies produced cheap cosmetics that working women could afford. Alongside the department stores' make-up counters, beauty parlours opened. Suddenly, make-up was big business – and so it would remain.

World War I was the first time many women began to work outside the home.

Make-up departments have a prominent position in modern department stores.

[33]

HOORAY FOR
- HOLLYWOOD -

During the 1930s and 1940s, many women wanted to look like the Hollywood film stars. The first giant cosmetics firms promised to help them.

Actors and actresses had worn make-up on stage for thousands of years. The make-up helped to emphasize the expressions on their faces. As black-and-white films began to be made, suddenly actresses were projected on screens that made them appear 3 metres (10 feet) tall. They wore make-up to look good at such large sizes!

THE SILVER SCREEN

Everything about the film stars was larger than life – including their make-up. Stars such as Clara Bow wore dark make-up, with heavily lined eyes and dark cupid-bow shaped lips, which worked well on screen. Women tried to copy the look. They flocked to the beauty salons of new cosmetics companies such as Elizabeth Arden, Helena Rubenstein and Max Factor.

Alice Joyce was a film star of the 1910s and 1920s.

[34]

ESCAPE FROM REALITY

When the **Great Depression** began in 1929, life became tough for many people. One of the most popular ways to escape from real life was a trip to the cinema. Watching glamorous film stars with their immaculate make-up inspired women to treat themselves when they could. These small treats helped keep up their spirits. In London, 1,500 times more lipsticks were sold in 1931 than had been sold a decade earlier.

Make-up gave people a chance to recreate a little of the glamour of stars such as Jean Harlow.

hello beautiful

Marlene Dietrich (right) and Greta Garbo were Hollywood stars famous for their beauty. Garbo was the first star to use a line of kohl to emphasize her eyes. Dietrich made her own kohl from the head of a burned match that she mixed with oil. Both stars' eyebrows were thin and arched and started a huge fashion trend.

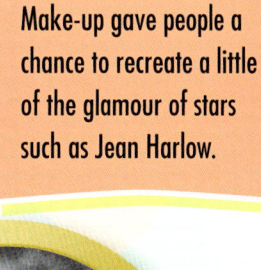

[35]

AVON - CALLING! -

In 1886 a man launched a new service that transformed how women bought make-up. It also gave lots of women a career.

David McConnell sold books door-to-door in New York, USA. He began giving housewives a free perfume sample so they would agree to listen to him. He soon noticed that his customers were not interested in the books – they just wanted the perfume.

HOME-SALES SUCCESS

McConnell launched the California Perfume Company (renamed Avon in 1939). McConnell's company was the world's first home-selling make-up business. When it started in 1886, women were reluctant to buy make-up from a shop. Make-up was still seen as being scandalous. Only a few years earlier, a Madame Rachel of Bond Street in London had **blackmailed** women who bought face powders from her.

Teenagers take lessons in how to apply make-up in the 1950s.

ON YOUR DOORSTEP

McConnell's genius was to allow women to buy products in the privacy of their homes. This was especially important in a period when the fear of social disapproval generally mattered more than it does today. McConnell also realized that women would probably buy more from a woman than a man. He persuaded a New Hampshire widow called Mrs Albee to work for him. She became the very first Avon lady. Many thousands of others followed her into selling make-up. Today, Avon's sales are falling. This reflects a different world. For many modern women, part of the fun of buying new make-up is trying it out with the help of an expert at a beauty counter in a department store.

Despite changing markets, Avon still has branches around the world.

to die for

In 1906, the African American Sarah Breedlove Davis opened a business selling her own hair products and cosmetics. She used the name Madam C.J. Walker, which she thought sounded French. Unlike most cosmetics, hers did not try to lighten black skin. Walker's skill at marketing made her one of the first successful African American entrepreneurs – and a millionaire.

POWER
- OF POP -

Make-up and rock and roll go together like fish and chips. And some male rock stars have worn far more make-up than women!

When Little Richard had a hit with "Tutti Frutti" in 1956, he was in full make-up. The singer used flamboyant eyeliner, eyebrow pencil and lip colour – and changed the face of rock and roll.

ON STAGE

Rock stars who followed in the 1960s often wore make-up, including the Rolling Stones' Mick Jagger. Wearing make-up on stage really took off in the 1970s with David Bowie. Bowie's painted appearance paved the way for later male stars such as Alice Cooper and Prince.

Each member of the rock band Kiss has his own black-and-white make-up design.

to die for

Goth music had its own look. Goths painted their faces white and then wore heavy make-up, from highly painted eyebrows to thick eye make-up and lips that could be any colour from black to white. The Goth make-up look was stylized, polished and edgy – and went perfectly with the dark Goth music.

CHANGES OF STYLES

For the Punks of the late 1970s, make-up was almost as important as music. Punks favoured a hard, aggressive look. That meant lots of black eyeliner and lip colour, together with many face piercings. Many also dyed their hair bright colours. Skin was usually pale, although that was often caused by an unhealthy lifestyle rather than make-up. The New Romantics of the 1980s preferred a painted face. They often whitened their faces to resemble Japanese geisha. Bands such as Duran Duran saw their faces as canvases on which to paint. Solo artist Adam Ant copied Native American warpaint.

Singer Amy Winehouse used kohl to enlarge her eyes and had a retro "beehive" hairstyle. This was originally a 1960s look.

[39]

Chapter 6
THE TWENTY-FIRST
- CENTURY -

Today, the beauty industry is a global business worth billions of pounds. With sophisticated advertising campaigns and marketing, it reaches everywhere.

In 1918, Max Factor came up with the Color Harmony Revolution. He was the first man to realize that different palettes of make-up would go better with different colours of hair. Make-up has come a long way since then. There is now make-up for every ethnic group, for different ages and for both sexes.

TRENDING TODAY

Modern make-up is so hi-tech that its ingredients resemble something from a chemistry lab. Japanese innovators led the way in high-tech make-up by experimenting with colour and texture in the late 1900s. Today, British and US make-up brands use chemicals that are more typically found in medicine or car paint, such as **silicone** and **mica**. Since the late 1990s, silicone oil has often been added to make-up to make it last longer.

Some women rarely leave the house without at least a bit of make-up.

[40]

Mica is a sparkling mineral that gives a new car its added sparkle – and also makes eye shadow appear to shimmer.

TOMORROW'S MEN

Many modern men are just as concerned about their appearance as previous generations of men have been throughout history. Like men from earlier times, some are experimenting with wearing make-up, including eyeliner, eye shadow, lipstick and face powder.

In Victorian England, men wore more make-up than women, but in the early twentieth century male make-up became **taboo**. When rock stars first started to wear make-up on stage in the 1960s and 1970s, there was public outrage. Today, male grooming is such big business that make-up has come full circle.

Cosmetic companies are starting to create make-up lines just for men. The next big thing in male make-up is predicted to be men-only make-up counters in department stores. Perhaps the dandy will be back in fashion again!

Male grooming is a rapidly growing market for cosmetics firms.

WHAT'S
- INSIDE? -

Like the first make-up, modern make-up uses natural ingredients. But some of these ingredients are actually quite disgusting!

Manufacturers set out to develop products that last and that are easy to apply. Making lipsticks from castor oil and wax does not make financial sense in the modern marketplace, because such ingredients go off quickly. Unexpected ingredients that appear in make-up today include fish scales, grease from sheep's wool and whale vomit!

YUCK!

Beauty companies spend millions of pounds on research and development. They try out new and unusual ingredients. A substance called ambergris, for example, is a very expensive ingredient used in perfume. It is actually protective oil from a whale's belly that the whale has thrown up. It is called ambergris because the name sounds a lot better than whale vomit!

A lipstick slides on easily because it contains fatty cells from sheep and other woolly mammals.

IT CONTAINS WHAT?

Lanolin is a standard ingredient in modern make-up. It helps products such as lipstick and eye shadow glide on. This is because lanolin is made from wax and dead fatty cells secreted by woolly mammals, such as sheep. Another revolting product that used to be common in eye make-up and lipstick is squalene, a gooey oil taken from the livers of sharks. Although squalene is no longer used, parts of other fish are. Fish scales add a sheen to nail polish. The scales are scraped off a dead fish, suspended in alcohol, then used to make cosmetics. At least fish scales are not toxic! Perhaps the age of terrible and toxic make-up is finally over.

Fish scales help make nail polish sparkle – like the fish themselves.

to die for

One fashion that seems to have died is Japanese tooth blackening. The Japanese once saw black teeth as a sign of beauty. To stain their teeth, the Japanese dissolved iron filings and **tannins** from tea in vinegar. They painted the resulting mixture on their teeth. The Japanese believed that black teeth warded off evil spirits and brought good luck.

[43]

-TIMELINE-

c. 50,000 BC — Neanderthals use shells as holders for pigments used as make-up.

c. 4000 BC — Cosmetics are in widespread use in Sumer and ancient Egypt.

c. 1500 BC — Women in China and Japan begin to paint their faces white and paint their teeth black or gold.

c. 1330 BC — Queen Nefertiti is a beauty icon in ancient Egypt.

c. 1200 BC — Assyrian women wear veils, while warriors wear make-up to go into battle.

c. 900 BC — The Phoenician princess Jezebel becomes renowned for her fashionable clothes and painted face.

500s BC — The ancient Greeks adopt a modest, natural-looking appearance for women.

69 BC — Cleopatra is born in Egypt; she will become a famous beauty of the ancient world.

AD 1 — Make-up is so common in Rome that the writer Plautus comments, "A woman without paint is like food without salt."

AD 476 — The Roman Empire is overthrown by Germanic peoples, and cosmetics largely disappear from Europe.

1028 — Empress Zoe becomes ruler of the Byzantine Empire; she protects her skin by never going outside.

1095 — The First Crusade begins as Christians fight Muslims for control of the Holy Land; Crusaders returning to Europe bring make-up and other fashions from Asia.

c. 1560 — Queen Elizabeth I begins a fashion of using white face powder.

1616	A British visitor criticizes the widespread use of face patches in Berlin.
c.1700	Geisha bring the fashion for white faces to a peak of popularity in Japan.
1764	Madame de Pompadour is said to apply rouge on her deathbed.
1774	Marie Antoinette becomes queen of France. She is noted for her extravagant appearance.
c.1785	Beau Brummel becomes leader of the dandies in London.
1789	After the French Revolution, royalty and the nobles lose their role as leaders of fashion.
1837	Victoria becomes queen of Britain. Despite being a noted beauty in her youth, she later turns against the use of cosmetics.
1840s	Chemists in the United States increasingly employ cosmeticians.
1867	The B. Altman department store in New York, USA, introduces the first "making-up" department.
1884	Guerlain in France makes the first commercial lipstick.
1886	US salesman David McConnell founds a door-to-door company selling make-up. It later becomes known as Avon.
1918	Max Factor introduces the Color Harmony Revolution, matching make-up tones to the colour of a woman's hair.
1920s	Young women known as Flappers wear make-up and have their hair cut short.
1956	Singer Little Richard has his first hit. He performs in full make-up.
1989	Men's make-up begins to become more popular.
2006	For his spring/summer fashion show, designer John Galliano makes up his models with white faces.

GLOSSARY

antimony silver-white semi-metal
arsenic highly poisonous element
blackmailed demanded money in return for not revealing damaging information
ceruse pigment or cosmetic made from white lead
coiffing styling or arranging hair
commercial related to buying and selling of goods
cosmetics substances that are applied to the skin, especially the face, to improve the appearance
courtiers people at a royal court who act as companions to a king or queen
dandies men who pay excessive attention to their appearance
disreputable having a reputation for poor character and morals
Flappers fashionable young women in the 1920s who broke the rules of accepted behaviour and appearance
Goth style of rock music with dark lyrics
Great Depression worldwide period of economic slowdown and high unemployment in the 1930s
imported shipped goods from one country into another
kimono long, loose Japanese robe
kohl black powder widely used as eye make-up in the ancient world
lead soft, heavy metal
lead carbonate white salt made from lead and carbon dioxide

leeches bloodsucking worms used in some medical treatments
manganese hard grey metal
mica shiny mineral found in rocks
minerals natural non-organic substances such as crystals and salts
Neolithic relating to the later part of the Stone Age, when people used weapons and tools
ochre earthy pigment that usually contains clay
oppression situation in which people are denied their rights
Pre-Raphaelite member of a group of nineteenth-century English artists who tried to paint simply, like painters in the early Renaissance
resin sticky substance released from the bark of some trees
rituals solemn religious ceremonies
rouge red powder or cream used to colour the cheeks or lips
saffron orange-yellow colouring made from crocus flowers
silicone artifical substance used to make rubber and plastics
taboo socially unacceptable
tannins bitter-tasting substances that occur in some plants
toxic poisonous
vain having excessive pride in one's own appearance
veils pieces of fine material worn by women to cover their faces

[46]

FIND OUT MORE

BOOKS

Body Pro: Facts and Figures About Bad Hair Days, Blemishes and Being Healthy (Girlology), Erin Falligant (Raintree, 2019)

A History of Britain in 12 Fashion Items, Paul Rockett (Franklin Watts, 2018)

Music, Fashion and Style (The Music Scene), Matthew Anniss (Franklin Watts, 2015)

Special Effects Make-up Artist (The Coolest Jobs on the Planet), Jonathan Craig and Bridget Light (Raintree, 2014)

WEBSITES

www.dkfindout.com/uk/history/fashion
Find out more about fashion through the ages.

www.dkfindout.com/uk/history/tudors/tudor-make-up
Find out more about Tudor make-up.

-INDEX-

Antoinette, Marie 22, 23, 45

Breedlove Davis, Sarah 37
Brummel, Beau 26, 28, 45
Byzantine Empire 15, 44

ceruse 17
  Venetian 20, 21
cheeks 7, 10, 12, 18, 22, 23
China 24, 44
cosmetics companies
  Avon 36–37, 45
  Elizabeth Arden 34
  Guerlain 31, 45
  Helena Rubenstein 34
  Max Factor 34, 45
creams 9, 29
Crusades 15, 44

dandies 26, 28–29, 41, 45
de' Medici, Catherine 15
de Pompadour, Madame 23, 45

early societies 6–7
  Assyrians 7
  Egyptians 6, 8–9
  Minoans 7
  Romans 7
  Sumerians 6, 7
England 16, 21, 26, 41, 44
eyes 6, 7, 8, 11, 24, 27, 34, 35, 38, 41, 43
  eyebrows 9, 17, 21, 24, 25, 28, 35, 38

Flappers 32, 33, 45
France 15, 18, 19, 22–23, 26, 45

geisha 24–25, 39, 43, 45

hair 22, 28, 40, 45
  beards 7, 15, 29
Hollywood 34–35

ingredients, make-up 5, 6, 7, 8, 9, 10, 11, 12, 17, 21, 25, 27, 30, 31, 40, 41, 42–43

Japan 24–25, 43, 44, 45
Jezebel 11, 44

kohl 7, 8, 9, 17, 35

lips 6, 17, 24, 34
  colour 6, 10, 17, 38, 39
  lipstick 9, 22, 25, 31, 32, 35, 41, 42, 43, 45

McConnell, David 36–37, 45
men and make-up, 8, 11, 12, 18, 22, 26, 28–29, 38, 39, 41, 45
mirrors 7, 9, 10, 15, 16
music and make-up 38–39, 41, 45

nails 9, 43

patches 19, 45
perfume 7, 12, 14, 20, 22, 23, 36, 42
Peru 12
poison 8, 9, 20, 21, 27, 43
  Aqua Tofana 21
powder 5, 8, 9, 21, 22, 25, 27, 30, 41, 44

queens
  Boudicca 12
  Cleopatra 8, 10, 44
  Elizabeth I 16–17, 18, 44
  Nefertiti 8
  Victoria 26, 27, 30, 32, 45

Roman Empire 11, 44
rouge 7, 11, 15, 18, 23, 24, 27, 28, 45
royalty 16–17

skin
  damage 17, 20, 25
  pale 7, 15, 17, 28, 30, 39
  white 9, 21, 24, 39, 44
stores, department 27, 45
  B. Altman 27, 45
  make-up counters 33, 37, 41
Sumer 7, 44

tattoos 5
teeth, blackened 24, 43, 44
toxins *see also* poison 20, 21, 43

United States 13, 27, 29, 32, 33

veils 12, 15, 44
Venice 20–21
Versailles 22, 23

war paint 7, 12–13, 44
wigs 16, 17
World War I 33

Zoe, Empress 15, 44

[48]